MW01421598

THE SIMPLE GUIDE TO

AUSTRALIA

CUSTOMS AND ETIQUETTE

COVER ILLUSTRATION

Sydney Opera House and replica of Captain Bligh's *Bounty*.
Photo: Courtesy Image Bank

ABOUT THE AUTHOR

ANGELA MILLIGAN specializes in training individuals and families for expatriate life. She has a particular interest in the countries where she has lived – Japan, Korea, Australia and Belgium. During her time in Australia, Angela lived and worked in Sydney and Melbourne; she also travelled extensively throughout the country observing life and customs both in cities and in the bush.

Her own experiences of being an expatriate have been incorporated in *How to Survive in Style* – a practical reference guide designed for newly-arrived expatriates to Britain.

Angela holds a degree in History from the University of East Anglia and is a Fellow of the Royal Society of Arts.

ILLUSTRATED BY
PETER SEARLE

SIMPLE GUIDE TO

AUSTRALIA

CUSTOMS & ETIQUETTE

ANGELA MILLIGAN

GLOBAL BOOKS LTD

Simple Guides • Series 1
CUSTOMS & ETIQUETTE

The Simple Guide to
AUSTRALIA
CUSTOMS & ETIQUETTE
by Angela Milligan

First published 2000 by
GLOBAL BOOKS LTD
PO Box 219, Folkestone, Kent, England CT20 3LZ

ISBN 1-86034-061-X

British Library Cataloguing in Publication Data
A CIP catalogue entry for this book
is available from the British Library

Set in Futura 11 on 12 pt by Bookman, Hayes, Middlesex
Printed in Malta by Interprint Ltd

Contents

This book is dedicated
to Robert, Pippa and
my many Australian friends

Time Line

1770 Captain Cook lands at Botany Bay and calls the Eastern coastline New South Wales

1788 First Fleet arrives

1793 First free settlers

1803 Matthew Flinders circumnavigates mainland

1840 Abolition of convict transportation to New South Wales

1845 Limited self government in New South wales

1851 Gold first discovered in New South Wales

1861 McDouall Stuart discovers centre of Australia

1876 Death of Truganini, last Tasmanian Aboriginal

1900 Federation of Australian Colonies. Melbourne chosen as temporary capital

1908 Canberra chosen as permanent capital

1915 Gallipoli campaign

1928 Royal Flying Doctor Service established

1932 Sydney Harbour Bridge opened

1942 Darwin bombed by Japanese

1947 Drive for immigration begins

1948 Qantas (Queensland and Northern Territories Airline System), the national airline, established

1956 Melbourne Olympic Games

1965 Australian troops sent to Vietnam

1966 Decimalization introduced

1966 Aborigines given full civic rights

1972 'White Australia' policy officially ended

1973 Sydney Opera House opened

1975 Whitlam Government dismissed by Governor-General

1983 Bob Hawke elected Prime Minister (continuous Labour Governments until 1996)

1991 Prime Minister Keating proposes of a republic

1998 Constitutional Conference on Republic

1999 Referendum on Republic (*See p. 31*)

2000 Sydney Olympic Games

'Advance Australia Fair'

AUSTRALIA'S NATIONAL ANTHEM SINCE
APRIL 1984

Australians all let us rejoice,
For we are young and free;
We've golden soil and wealth for toil;
Our home is girt by sea;
Our land abounds in nature's gifts
Of beauty rich and rare;
In history's page, let every stage
Advance Australia Fair.
In joyful strains then let us sing,
Advance Australia Fair.

Beneath our radiant Southern Cross
We'll toil with hearts and hands;
To make this Commonwealth of ours
Renowned of all the lands;
For those who've come across the seas
We've boundless plains to share;
With courage let us all combine
To Advance Australia Fair.
In joyful strains then let us sing,
Advance Australia Fair.

Australia – a Very Special Place

Bowls near Sydney Harbour Bridge

Australia (Terra Australis) or Great Southern Land is unique – a large country, an island and a continent. It is a country the same size as the United States of America, spanning three time zones, yet its population is barely 18 million. It is an

Map of Australia

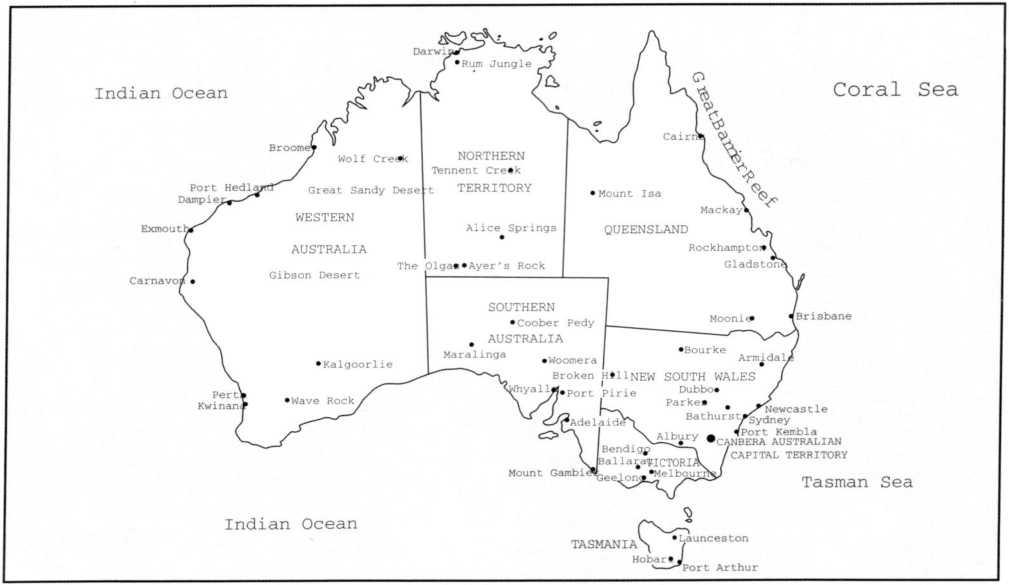

ancient land with an ancient people: the Aboriginal and Torres Strait Islanders. A land of vast contrasts: deserts, snowy mountains, temperate lush valleys and rolling fields, bush, ancient rain forest and the Great Barrier Reef.

There is nothing average about Australia. The climate varies from torrential rain to terrible drought with the ever-present threat of bush fires and the country's native animal, plant and bird life has been driven by these extremes. This, together with the relative isolation of Australia for 50 million years, has produced a rich and diverse environment.

Kangaroos (of various sizes and colour), wallabies, platypus, echidna, galahs, kookaburras, koalas and brightly-coloured parrots are some of the more famous species which will entrance the visitor. Even the ubiquitous gum or eucalyptus tree contains a surprise for it is actually dependent on fire for its survival and propagation.

But, despite its vast size, almost 4,000 kilometres from east to west and 3,000 kilometres from north to south, most of the population lies on the coastal fringe, for the Australian interior is an inhospitable place: a semi-desert, extremely hot in summer and with temperatures occasionally falling below zero on winter nights.

Australia's cities are vibrant, cosmopolitan places, distinctive in character and proud of their identity from the historic first colonial settlement of Sydney with its famous Harbour Bridge and Opera House to the frontier feel of Darwin. Elsewhere the wide elegant streets and imposing nineteenth-century buildings of sophisticated Melbourne are very different from the purpose-built capital of Canberra with its award-winning Parliament building.

German architecture and culture are most prominent in the graceful city of Adelaide; whereas Hobart, the capital of Australia's smallest state, Tasmania, across the Bass Strait, has an old-fashioned charm with its splendid, well-preserved Georgian buildings, neatly laid out streets, stone churches and pretty gardens.

Perth, the modern dynamic city of soaring skyscrapers in Western Australia, focuses on the outdoor life, as does Brisbane, capital of the 'sunshine state' of Queensland, with its glorious climate. This vast state covers the top right-hand corner of Australia and is traditionally where many Australians take their beach and island holidays.

Hot Tip: 'No Worries Mate!'

Because so much of Australia's population live within twenty kilometres of the ocean, together with the fact that the winters are short and mild, explains the laid-back, outdoor life-style with its emphasis on sport. 'No worries mate!'

A fluid culture means that there is something for everyone. The arts scene is extensive and vibrant, ranging from jazz and rock festivals to the splendid seasons of opera, ballet and classical music. The large museums regularly mount international exhibitions and the galleries are proud of their collections of colonial, modern and Aboriginal art – the latter thanks to the American-Australian scientific expedition to Arnhem Land in the far north in 1948, where Aboriginal works were widely collected for their artistic and aesthetic merit. Indeed, it is Aboriginal art which is the key to understanding this unique culture. All the state galleries contain important collections of Aboriginal art and make a most rewarding visit.

Australian film and theatre are alive and well and while many visitors will be familiar with the successful products of the former such as *Picnic at Hanging Rock*, the moving First World War epic *Gallipoli*, *My Brilliant Career* and the light-hearted *Muriel's Wedding*, few will be aware that there is a thriving theatre from experimental to Open-Air Shakespeare, with possums sometimes taking an unscripted part!

For the discerning and adventurous eater a vast cornucopia of delights awaits. The new style of Australian cooking is exciting and not conditioned by tradition and custom. Helped by excellent, easily available local produce and a simplicity of approach, Australian chefs mix ingredient and style in an unorthodox fashion, thus creating what might be described as Pacific Fusion cuisine.

In the Austalian kitchen Thailand, Japan and Italy happily sit together on a plate for either lunch or dinner and there are many combinations of this partnership including influences from other Pacific Rim countries as well as those of Southern Europe such as Provence and Greece. The food is further enhanced by the wide choice of remarkable wines that the country has produced in recent years.

Hot Tip: 'It Doesn't Get Better Than This!'

It would be a rare visitor who was not amazed and intrigued at times at Australia's diversity, even the native swans are black. As the Aussies succinctly put it: 'It doesn't get better than this!'

The Jumper!

2

Understanding the History

Captain Philip arrives with the 'First Fleet' at Port Jackson, Sydney, January 1788

This is not intended to be a definitive history of Australia but rather to give the visitor some understanding and historical perspective of Australian society and the challenges that face that society today.

Australia has a long history of Aboriginal settlement, at least 50,000 years, but tragically European colonization all but wiped out the indigenous population and their unique culture. They were seen as nomadic people not agrarian and, consequently, Australia was declared to be 'empty', ready in other words for exploitation. A historic view that was to have far-reaching and terrible consequences that the early settlers of the eighteenth century never foresaw. That view taken two hundred years ago is causing major constitutional problems in Australia today.

Historically, the Spanish, the Dutch and the French were all at some time interested in Australia, but it was the British who were to be the European colonizers. Apart from the scientific community, there had been little British interest in Captain James Cook's voyages on the *Endeavour* in 1770, but all that was to change dramatically after the loss of the American colonies in 1783.

One of the immediate outcomes was the problem of what to do with the increasing prison population that had previously been transported to the Americas. The gaols were at bursting point and as a temporary measure rotting hulks moored on the River Thames were used as overflow accommodation. A more permanent solution had to be found and quickly and so it was that the British Prime Minister of the day, William Pitt, and his cabinet saw Australia as the answer to the country's penal problems.

Ignoring the Aboriginal population, all the government of the day could envisage was a vast, open, 'empty' country, ripe for settlement and, above all, remote from Britain.

'THE FIRST FLEET'

So it was that in 1787, on 13 May, Captain Arthur Philip set sail with a small complement of eleven ships from Portsmouth. Not all the names of the ships or those on board are known, but the whole enterprise was to be known thereafter as 'The First Fleet'. On board were about 750 convicted felons, many of whom had committed such inhuman crimes as the woman who had stolen 12lbs of cheese. None had committed murder, their crimes were against property (stealing a sheep was a hanging offence) and for this the sentences were reduced to transportation for life to Australia.

The Fleet consisted of around six hundred men, in addition to the convicts, plus fifty women and children of officers' families. Having rejected Botany Bay where Cook had landed, Philip sailed on to Port Jackson, or Sydney Cove as it was to become known. He landed on 26 January 1788, an event that is commemorated today as Australia Day.

The early years were difficult ones for the new penal settlement, starvation being a continual threat. As there was little or no contact with the Aboriginal people, the new arrivals were ignorant of the fruits, seeds and nuts surrounding them in the bush as well as the abundant supply of meat and game, albeit of a very different kind from their diet in Britain. Furthermore, they found both the soil too hard to plough and much of the timber too tough to fell. By 1790 the situation was so serious that a large proportion of the settlement was moved to Norfolk Island – about 1,500 kilometres to the east.

Philip decided on radical action to solve the combined problems of food shortage and the ravages of drought: parcels of land were duly given to former convicts, who were to be known as 'emancipists'. At the same time a Second Fleet was dispatched from Britain, containing both free women and female convicts, as it was hoped that the influence of the women would help civilize the settlement. It is worth noting that out of a total of 1,000 convicts, 267 died on this long, terrible voyage.

FIRST 'FREE SETTLERS'

Philip departed in 1792 and in the following year the first Free Settlers arrived. Few convict ships came in the next twelve years as Britain and Europe were immersed in the Napoleonic wars and there was a continual shortage of enlisted men, in both the army and navy. As well as free men being 'pressed' into service, prisoners were seen as likely fodder for the army, what the Duke of Wellington was later to refer to as 'the scum of the earth'.

These events gave the settlement in Australia, now known as New South Wales, a breathing space in which to establish itself. A momentous decision was also taken to import Merino sheep from South Africa. Australia is said to have ridden on the sheep's back ever since!

As well as Philip, the early governors were for their time far-sighted men and none more so than Governor Macquarie. Indeed, he is often referred to as 'The Father of Australia'. He arrived after a mutiny and the overthrow of the previous governor. The military had become rich and powerful, due to their access to free land and cheap labour but the arrival of Lachlan Macquarie with his own forces was to finish that.

PRISONERS' RIGHTS

Macquarie improved conditions for the prisoners, supported their right to become free citizens once they had finished their sentences, appointed many to public office and made use of the talents of these former convicts, such as the architect Francis Greenaway.

Between 1809 and 1821, the period of Macquarie's governship there were many fine buildings erected including the 'Rum Hospital'. Macquarie was denied funds from London for his grand projects and so the hospital and other buildings were built on the proceeds of the sale of alcohol. The hospital is one of the earliest buildings in Australia and now houses the New South Wales

Parliament. He and his wife designed it and Elizabeth Macquarie is also remembered today by many travellers who visit her 'chair' which she had carved out of rock, from which point you can survey the harbour.

A THRIVING COLONY

It was not long before the settlement was thriving and attracting many voluntary immigrants from Britain and Ireland, laying the foundations of an Anglo-Celtic society, which was to prevail until the mid-1870s. By 1819, in fact, New South Wales was the main destination for overseas emigration from the British Isles.

However, there was soon tension between the emancipists and the voluntary immigrants or 'squatocracy' (landowner squatters) who thought that the ex-convicts were being granted too many favours and so to ease this problem the next governor, Thomas Brisbane, used convicts to colonize other areas of Australia such as Tasmania,

An 'outback' landscape

Queensland and Western Australia. New South Wales itself attained the status of a colony in 1823 and so the die was cast for the new country.

The great race now began to find the centre of Australia. In 1803 Matthew Flinders had circumnavigated the coast, but the vast hinterland had gone unexplored. After an earlier abortive attempt, Melbourne was founded in 1834 and Adelaide two years later. It was from Adelaide that Charles Sturt set off on his ill-fated attempt to try and cross the centre of Australia. However, the great heat and subsequent ill health put an end to the expedition. Burke and Wills stirred the public's imagination when they crossed from Melbourne in the south to the Gulf of Carpentaria in the far north, but the centre was finally reached by John McDouall Stuart. It was a bittersweet discovery, dashing all hopes of finding lush rolling pastures and an inland sea, for it was dry, infertile and inhospitable land.

MINERAL DISCOVERIES

As well as breath-taking, geographical discoveries there were important mineral discoveries being made, which were to lay the foundations of Australia's future prosperity. John Askew writing in 1857 about the area of Newcastle in New South Wales, commented that '. . . the coal mines of the district bid fair to become as important as those of our own far-famed Newcastle. The coal field extends over hundreds of square miles and is all but inexhaustible.'

But it was the discovery of gold, firstly in New South Wales and then Victoria that stirred the public's imagination and that of the world. The gold rush led to a mini-boom, but few, however, made their fortunes. A visit to the former gold fields at Ballarat in Victoria, will illustrate the hope, despair, hard work and privation that the miners faced. Furthermore, there was clear discrimination in the way the licences were awarded.

Finally, tempers erupted and the miners defied the authorities by building barricades at Eureka near Ballarat. They stood their ground despite being charged by armed militia and eventually all their demands were met, including the right to vote. This event has been seen as a turning point in Australian history, one that helped shape the nation's character.

Mining for gold in New South Wales

Hot Tip: 'Jack is as Good as his Master'

It could be argued that Australia's belief in equality and dislike of authority together with the philosophy that 'Jack is as good as his master' was determined by events that played themselves out on the desolate gold fields at Eureka.

Later, in the 1920s when D. H. Lawrence visited Australia and wrote *Kangaroo*, he observed that whereas some people felt 'better off' than others, nobody felt 'better' than anyone else. Perhaps, too, because of the appalling working conditions that they had left behind in Britain and Ireland that the 'new' Australians won basic rights amazingly early on, including the eight-hour working day in 1855.

CONSTITUTIONAL DECISIONS

As the nineteenth century drew to a close, Australians began to consider their constitutional future. Their penal origins were well behind them. Indeed, transportation was abandoned in 1852, for it did not seem appropriate to send criminals for punishment to a country where others were desperate to go for land, work and gold. However much though the colonies disliked government from London, they were suspicious of each other and worried by the prospect of a central government, which might appropriate their mineral resources. Eventually, federation was seen as the only way forward and just as the First Fleet arrived in January, so the Commonwealth of Australia was born on 1 January 1901.

It could be argued that for a nation of 18 million people, Australia today is the most governed country in the world, at least it has the most layers of government per head of population. The federal government is based in Canberra with a prime minister and parliament based on the Westminster system. Parliament is composed of two houses, the House of Representatives and the Senate and both are elected. All states have equal representation in the Senate to balance the power of the larger states in the House of Representatives. The British monarch, as head of state, is represented by the Governor-General and the states all have their own parliaments and premiers, first minister of the state, and a governor, representing the Governor-General. To maintain the checks and balances in this system a High Court was established. There are city, local and shire councils in each state as well.

Hot Tip: Voting is Mandatory

To counteract any feelings of political apathy in Australia and because of the small population, it is mandatory to vote in General Elections, which have to be called at least every three years.

'WHITE AUSTRALIA'

In its first two years the new Federal Government passed two momentous pieces of legislation. The first was the infamous 'White Australia' Act.

Racial tension had first reared its ugly head in the gold fields and the rights and privileges that had been won at Eureka did not extend to the many Chinese workers who had arrived in the 1850s.

The Chinese grew prosperous not so much by digging for gold, but by being far-sighted enough to establish local stores and market gardens, thereby supplying the miners with provisions in a harsh environment. However, there was little regard for this on the miners' side and soon the flames of jealousy were fanned, especially as the Chinese sometimes found gold in abandoned claims. Riots broke out, the most serious at Lambing Flats in 1861. Atrocities were committed and the military were sent in, but despite arresting the perpetrators, they were freed by an all-white jury.

Similar incidents happened when Solomon Islanders were brought to Queensland to work in the sugar fields. By the end of the nineteenth century, feelings of insecurity, plus the possibility of being swamped by their Asian neighbours, led to the 'White Australia' immigration bill being rushed into law in 1901.

In the following year, the Federal Parliament showed itself to be in reforming mood when women were granted the vote. Although this is early in European and American terms, their sisters across the Tasman Sea in New Zealand had been granted the franchise in 1897.

WAR AND DEPRESSION

The Federation was only a few years old when it was swept up by world events. Australians were anxious to come to the aid of what they still regarded as the mother country when the First World War broke out in 1914. Large numbers volunteered and were promptly sent to the battle-fields of northern France.

While en route the Australian troops were diverted by the British Government to Turkey and bravely, but vainly, attempted to establish a new front at Gallipoli, for Turkey had entered the war on the German side in 1916. Thousands of Australian soldiers or 'diggers' as they have affectionately become known were mown down by Turkish gun emplacements. Yet this terrible tragedy, never forgotten, was to enter the consciousness of Australia, forging the spirit of the country and further underlining the ordinary 'Aussies' dislike of British authority.

Australia, like the rest of the world, was plunged into depression between the two world wars as it found the overseas markets for its agricultural products collapsing. Furthermore, a growing divide between urban and rural Australia opened up, one that can be observed by the visitor today. Large public works were undertaken in order to alleviate unemployment, such as the building of Sydney's Harbour Bridge and the mighty 'Ghan' railway. The railway was so named after the turbaned and robed Afghan cameleers who, before roads or rail were in place, provided the only supply link to the middle of nowhere, trading their wares from the backs of the animals. Originally a narrow-gauge railway, it followed not only the line of the Afghan cameleers, but also that of John McDouall Stuart.

The Second World War, like the First, had a profound effect on the Australian identity, but this time Australia itself was faced with possible invasion, especially after the fall of Hong Kong, Singapore and Indonesia. The Japanese bombed Darwin, launched submarine raids against Sydney and Newcastle and invaded New Guinea, an Australian colony. The Government looked this time to the United States rather than Britain for help and the US military chose Australia as a base for coordinating the war effort in the Pacific.

Barnado boys arriving in Australia in 1924

THE POST-WAR WORLD

After the war, Australia realized that its future was much more bound up with events in both America and Asia rather than Europe and ties with the US were strengthened which would eventually lead to Australia participating in the Vietnam War.

The Second World War also made Australia realize that it would have to populate or perish and so began the huge flood of immigrants from war-torn Europe, especially southern Europe.

Hot Tip: The '£10 Pom'

After the Second World War a novel scheme to recruit migrants from Britain was introduced. Passages were subsidized and so was born the £10 Pom, the colloquial expression for the English supposedly after 'Prisoner of His Majesty'.

With the advent of a Labor Government in 1972 under the leadership of Gough Whitlam, the White Australian Policy was not only officially abandoned but Asian immigration especially promoted.

Today, Australia regards itself as a multi-cultural society, even though the extreme right wing has sought to challenge that image in the last few years. Its new cultural make-up is well on the way to cutting the last of the formal ties with Britain. Republican feelings were first stirred in recent times (there had been talk of this at the time of Federation in 1901) by the constitutional crisis of 1975, when the then Governor-General, Sir John Kerr, dismissed Prime Minister Whitlam and dissolved Parliament. Up until this point, the powers of the Governor-General, representing the British monarch, had never been so clearly expressed for he had always been regarded as a figurehead with only constitutional powers as a formality.

These events made all Australians think about the country's long-term constitutional position and with the election of Paul Keating as Prime Minister in 1991, who advocated that Australia became a republic by the year 2000, new voice was given to republican hopes. He and the Labor Party have since lost office, but even a Liberal Government was committed to holding a constitutional conference in 1998 and that in turn decided that a referendum on the issue of whether Australia should become a republic should be held in 1999.

The referendum resulted in a win for the monarchists, albeit by a narrow margin. The feeling in the country today is that a future referendum will indeed result in Australia becoming a republic.

Many older Australians, especially those who belong to the RSL (the Returned Services League, an ex-serviceman's association), are deeply worried by these events and do not want to lose the Queen of Australia. Furthermore, they fear that any attack on the monarchy will lead to the replacing of the Australian flag.

The Aboriginal Experience

Aboriginal art – 'The Lightning Man'

It is a sobering thought to realize that the Aboriginal people have been in Australia for at least 50,000 years and theirs is one of the world's oldest living cultures. Although the indigenous population was grouped together and termed 'Aboriginal' by the European colonizers, within that grouping there are many distinct tribes, customs and languages. Sadly, many of these tribes and languages have since died out, as the history of the Aboriginal people from 1788 onwards is often a tragic and traumatic one.

In the early years of colonization the Aboriginals were often treated as wild animals by the white man and hunted as such, even to extinction, as in Tasmania. Those who survived this onslaught fell prey to the new diseases of smallpox, measles, influenza, as well as that of perhaps the most deadly of all – alcohol.

When the First Fleet arrived there were approximately three-quarters of a million indigenous inhabitants, while today the numbers have dropped to around a third of that. A most moving and poignant testament to this, is the Aboriginal memorial in the National Gallery of Australia in Canberra. It is based on the Aboriginal burial ritual and is made up of hundreds of slender tree trunks, hollowed out by termites and painted with the emblems of the different Aboriginal tribes. Traditionally, when a person died, his or her bones were put inside similar trunks and left to the elements, thus ensuring the safe passage to the spirit world. The memorial was created in the bicentennial year of the 'discovery' of Australia and is the first item on display in the gallery.

From the beginning Australia was regarded by the Latin tag of '*terra nullius*', or empty land, and ripe for the taking. In contrast, for the Aboriginal people land is sacred and is a source of all life. For the elders of the tribes land is a valuable treasure, something that they are custodians of, having been handed down to them from the Dreaming Time or the Creation.

Many Aboriginal people feel linked to the land in a mystic way, for the place you were born in gives you your identity. Sharing the land and travelling across it are deeply instinctive, so, too, are its invisible workings. It is not difficult to see that Aboriginals and colonizers were on a collision path two hundred years ago and it remains a deeply sensitive issue in Australia today.

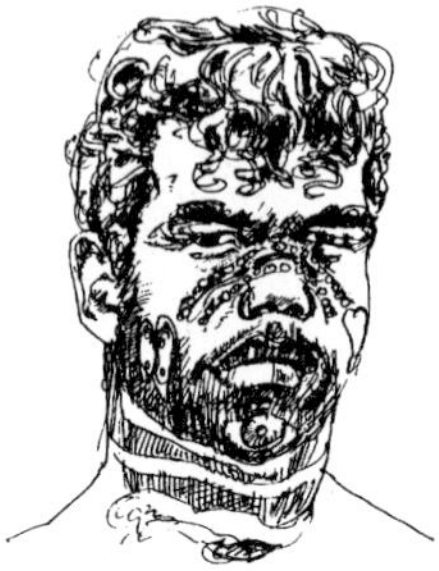

Aboriginal performer

In the nineteenth century it was the intoxicating, believable possibility of owning land that brought thousands of emigrants from Europe, as well as the post-war migrant settlement, exacerbating the plight of the Aboriginals.

In addition, there has been little or no allowance made for the very different psyche of the

Aboriginal people. Being nomadic they can disappear on 'walkabout' giving rise to the belief that they are 'unreliable' and that can equate to 'unemployable'. Again, the lie of the land and the vast open spaces they inhabited for thousands of years sometimes makes it difficult for Aboriginal people with a wide extended family, to settle down in a neat, suburban house. This sometimes leads to the view that they are 'ungrateful'. Furthermore, their long-held view about communal ownership is sometimes interpreted as 'untrustworthy'.

An insight into Aboriginal culture is to be found in an appreciation and understanding of their art. It is part of a living tradition, which is constantly changing and adapting to time. The earliest examples are found mainly on wood and bark, depicting stories about the land and the life-giving properties of water, for this is a land constantly plagued by drought.

The technique of dotting to create a shimmering effect, characteristic of many works, invests the art with a spiritual presence. In more recent years urban as well as themes from the bush have found expression with the use of canvas and acrylic paint.

Hot Tip: Secrets of the Bush

Nothing can quite explain the experience of listening to Aboriginal people, talking about the secrets of the bush and the ancient rain forest.

Many State Governments are actively encouraging indigenous tourism, ranging from accompanied guided tours to stays at Aboriginal-run lodges. Although still having a long way to go, recent improvements in health care and education have not only increased numbers especially among the urban Aboriginal population but also made the people more aware of their own culture as well as taking a renewed pride in it. Nothing illustrates this more than the emergence of many successful Aboriginal performance groups as well as the promotion of bush-flower remedies.

In 1967 Aboriginal people were given full civil rights, after a nation-wide referendum showed that 90% of the Australian population was overwhelmingly in favour of this. This attitude contrasted with that taken in the 1950s, when it was genuinely felt that by removing Aboriginal children from their parents and placing them with white families, or in orphanages, would be to their advantage and help to assimilate them. This period of Aboriginal history is a very painful one and has left both a deep scar and a feeling of humiliation.

Although in 1990 a government commission gave Aboriginal people control of the many federal-funded programmes directed at them, the heart of the problem is the legal position of the land. This has produced constitutional uproar, beginning with the 1992 judgement handed down by the High Court of Australia which dramatically overturned the concept that Australia was '*terra nullius*' in 1788. This, in turn, has sparked furious and continuing debate. No doubt this issue will run and run, but the visitor to Australia should be aware that while the topic of Aboriginal rights is not a taboo subject for discussion, it is a highly sensitive issue and one which engenders strong feelings.

Aboriginal fishermen

4

Tucker: Food & Drink

'Tinnies'

Australians are an informal, friendly people and easy to get to know. They display neither the British reserve nor the exuberant friendliness of the Americans. Theirs is something in between: a laid-back attitude, the take-it-or-leave-it variety, which is no doubt a result of the Australian climate.

Australians will want the visitor to enjoy their country as much as they do. It will not be long before the overseas guest is treated to Australian hospitality at either a BBQ, a 'barbie', or one of the many excellent restaurants that have sprung up in and around the main cities and towns.

Hot Tip: Modern Australian Cuisine

Australians are justly proud of their modern Australian cuisine, a far cry from the 'meat and two veg' variety of yesteryear. Today, a mixture of East and West and Aussie chefs are gaining a worldwide reputation for innovation.

The interest in food and the somewhat eclectic restaurant menus one finds everywhere are due to the many migrants who have arrived from all over the world and made Australia their home, bringing with them their traditions and recipes. Indeed, Australia owes a real debt to the Greek and Southern Italian immigrants who came after World War II, for not only did they bring with them their love of food, but also the Mediterranean cuisine.

Italians are the largest ethnic group after the predominantly Anglo-Celtic, while the number of first- and second-generation Greeks is said to make Melbourne the second largest Greek city in the world after Athens. More recently, Lebanese, Vietnamese, Indonesian, Indian, Thai and Chinese as well as people from the former country of Yugoslavia have settled and brought with them their culinary culture.

So everything and anything is available and both shopping for food in one or other of the large markets – as in Victoria Market in Melbourne – or one of the many splendid food halls – as in the David Jones' chain – or eating out at restaurants is a real delight and an eye-opener as to the breadth of choice on offer. Another way to experience this variety is to eat at one or more of the many popular food courts, an idea successfully borrowed from Singapore, that have become established in the basement of office blocks and shopping malls. There the diner can choose from a large display of Thai, Indonesian, Italian, Japanese and whatever other foods is on offer. This makes a deliciously different as well as reasonably-priced meal.

BUSH TUCKER

Australians since the first European settlers have largely been unaware of the abundance of food that surrounds them in the bush. However, the green debate, together with the growing preoccupation with health has made many people conscious of the healthy properties of an Aboriginal diet. Interest is growing in discovering the novel textures and flavours of native Australian plants, nuts and berries, while TV programmes featuring celebrity chefs, glossy magazine articles and numerous books are devoted to the subject.

Kangaroo, crocodile and emu are low in fat and cholesterol, but whether they can be described as bush tucker is debatable as many are raised on farms for the table. The witchetty grub is a different matter. It is an insect larva that can be eaten raw or cooked. As well as appearing on organized bush tours as a novelty, it is also making an appearance on the menus of smart restaurants. An acquired taste, that's for sure! Wattle seeds are perhaps easier for the novice!

WINE

Although the visitor may be familiar with Australian wines and their challenging bouquets and appealing taste, only a small proportion is exported – the Aussies keeping the best for themselves! Generally speaking Australians are well informed about their native wines and eager to discuss grape varieties, vintages and the new areas of the country under cultivation.

Hot Tip: Australia's Wine-producing Regions

Traditionally, the best wine-producing areas are in the Hunter Valley in New South Wales and the Barossa Valley in South Australia, but recently there have been great advances in wine production from as far north as Queensland down to Victoria, Tasmania and over to Western Australia.

If time allows, a visit to a winery, especially one of the smaller-run businesses or 'boutique' wineries, would be most rewarding as would a little reading (there are a vast number of books on the subject) and a sense of adventure.

Wine-tastings are usually free of charge, except for premium wines and even for these only a small fee is charged. Wines are for sale, although prices are no longer cheaper than the big retail outlets in the cities as they once were. However, if you are interested in taking some of the local wine with you as a reminder of your stay in Oz, many of the wineries will arrange shipment for you. But do remember the added cost of customs duties in your home country.

As well as the tastings on offer, many of the wineries are situated in beautiful locations, well worth a visit in their own right. Some even have their own restaurants and delight in matching the local produce with the wineries' specialities. Even in restaurants in towns and cities, Australia also has the wonderful practice in neighbourhood restaurants of BYO, or bring your own, allowing you to take in the wine of your choice; just check if this option is available when making the reservation.

'. . . well informed about native wines'

BEER

Before ordering a beer, a visitor would do well to be aware of the unique terminology used in Australia. First of all, measures are smaller than those served in Europe ranging from a 'middie' (half pint) to a schooner (about 15 oz.) and nothing to do with ships or drinking sherry! To confuse matters further some states have different names for these measures. In general, 'stubbies' are short-necked bottles and 'tinnies', as the name suggests, are cans of beer. Most importantly, the beer should be served cold and in order to keep it so, especially during the summer months and in the northern states all the year round, beer is served in a 'cooler' made from polystyrene. Each state has its own brewery, although many beers are sold nationwide.

Hot Tip: Caution: Strong Beer!

It is worth noting that regular Australian beers are considerably stronger than their US counterparts and also slightly stronger than the lagers sold in Britain. However, 'lite' beers or low alcohol beers are growing in popularity.

Be careful about possible confusion over the use of the word 'hotel' which is sometimes used to refer to a pub. However, there should be no confusion when it is your 'round' or 'shout', i.e., your turn to buy the drinks. You gain no popularity points in Oz by conveniently forgetting.

COFFEE & TEA

An excellent range of coffees and teas is available in Australia. Visitors from England, in particular, may be surprised to see everywhere the vast numbers of teashops serving 'Devonshire Teas' – complete with scones, cream and jam. Australians consume great quantities of these which have come to be regarded as something of a 'national' institution.

Tea has long been a popular beverage, due no doubt to the Anglo-Celtic influence. 'Morning' Tea is a ritual in many shops, offices and banks. A wide range of blends and varieties is available, including locally-grown and herbal teas.

Coffee, like beer, has developed a vocabulary all of its own. Thus, a 'coffee latte' is made with plenty of hot milk, either skinny (skimmed) or full-cream and served in a tall glass, while a 'flat white' is a plain white coffee and a regular black coffee is known as a 'long black'. A short black is an espresso, while a macchiato is an espresso with a little milk and a cappuccino is . . . a cappuccino.

Many cafés, usually run by Italian families, sell excellent cakes and pastries as well as tasty snacks and sandwiches freshly made to order. The shopping malls and arcades including the magnificent nineteenth-century ones are good spots to find these cafés and tea shops and watch the world go by. As in Europe you can take your time sipping your coffee and many cafés have newspapers and glossy magazines for the customer to browse through.

Glossary of Food Terms

Anzac Biscuits – Biscuits made from rolled oats, honey and syrup. They were sent to the Australian and New Zealand (Anzac) Troops at Gallipoli during World War I.

Balmain Bugs, Moreton Bay Bugs, Yabbies – A type of crayfish.

Damper – A flat bread baked in the embers of a fire.

Chiko Rolls – A deep-fried roll filled with potato, cabbage and gravy.

Aussie Floater – A meat pie in a large amount of gravy.

Pavlova – meringue filled with fruit and cream.

Vegemite – A strong, dark yeast sandwich and toast spread.

Lamington – A sponge cake covered in a thin layer of chocolate and rolled in desiccated coconut.

'Outdoor cooking'

5

Doing Business

Australian Stock Exchange, Sydney

Twenty years ago the phrases 'She'll be right' and 'God's lucky country' summed up not only the average Australian's attitude to social life, but business and work as well. Strikes and demarcation disputes were notorious, indeed a way of life, and some industries in addition to paid annual holiday entitlement had a leisure day a month as well. Time has brought about a change of attitude as Australia strives to remain competitive in world markets.

Australians of most political persuasion have long realized that the country's best interests are in defining itself as part of the Asia Pacific Region, although it is only fair to say that some of its Asian neighbours are not entirely convinced of this view. Australia also wants to upgrade its mix of exports in order to reduce the economy's reliance on its natural resources and the agricultural sector, important though these both are.

Personal relationships are important in doing business. Aggressive or high-pressure sales techniques, long-winded reports or detailed presentations are usually counter-productive. Australians appreciate openness and directness and brevity is admirable, as is punctuality, in a business setting. 'Cutting down the Tall Poppy' or deflating pomposity is a national pastime.

Hot Tip: A Sense of Humour is the Key!

Aussies are laconic with a well-developed sharp-edged sense of humour to match. Do not be offended, give as good as you get and above all keep your sense of humour! You will be respected for this.

As far as business dress is concerned, it is at its most formal, as perhaps are business meetings, in Adelaide and especially in Melbourne, while dress becomes more relaxed as one travels north. But however relaxed the setting and one's business colleagues, it is important to be prepared, equipped with business cards and fully briefed for business meetings because the law of the bottom line applies as much to Australia as anywhere else in the world. In addition, Australian business journalists are well informed and business journals and newspapers are widely read.

There is a wide share-owning population in Australia and the 1990s' privatization of some of the country's State-owned industries, such as telecoms and transportation, together with the flotation of several large companies has produced a huge response.

Business hours are usually 9.00am to 5.00pm Monday to Friday, while major department stores in the big cities usually have one late night shopping evening a week, very often on a Thursday or a Friday. Banks open from 9.00am to 4.00pm Monday to Thursday, with again a later closing time on Friday. Saturday is the principal shopping day, while Sunday is largely seen as a day of rest. In other words a day on the beach, or having a barbie, although shopping is on the increase.

Having the ability to relax and enjoy whatever business entertainment is provided is important, as it is an expression of interest in the country outside the area of business matters. If it is your first visit to Australia, you are certain to be asked what you think of the place, not just once, but by nearly all those you are introduced to.

To entertain (if appropriate) or to be entertained provides a very good opportunity for your business colleagues, or associates to get to know you and these occasions can often smooth the business path as well as help cement a business relationship. If entertaining a group, or where you want some privacy while discussing sensitive business issues, you might consider going to one of the many excellent Chinese restaurants and hiring a private dining room for lunch or dinner. All the big cities have excellent guides to eating out, which can easily be purchased in local bookshops.

It goes without saying that the mobile phone should not be used at the table, either to receive or make calls. If it is absolutely essential to make or take a call, do at least remove yourself from the table. Smoking is another sensitive issue. Be careful about lighting up either in a restaurant or private home without asking. If you do not see any ashtrays in the latter, then it is a safe bet that it is a non-smoking household and probably best to abandon the desire for a cigarette. Most non-smokers will only allow close relatives to smoke in their homes and sometimes not even then! Many restaurants are totally non-smoking and those that allow it usually have a certain designated area. If a table is not available in that area, then in Aussie speak 'you'll have to live with that' or go outside.

If at all possible, it is a good idea to visit Australia on business from March to November. Not only is the climate more temperate, but those times miss the main tourist season and holiday months. The long summer holiday is taken around December to January, when the schools are closed and the weather is at its hottest. It is also worth noting and avoiding the public and individual state holidays as many people take advantage of these breaks and often go away.

National Holidays

New Year's Day
Australia Day (nearest Monday to 26 January)
Good Friday
Easter Monday
Anzac Day (25 April)
Christmas Day
Boxing Day

Note: In addition to the above all states have their own special holidays
e.g. **Melbourne Cup Day** (first Tuesday in November), **Victoria Queen's Birthday** (first Monday in June)

Sydney Harbour Bridge

6

Contemporary Etiquette

'Table manners follow the British pattern'

It is good practice for the visitor in all countries to have an idea of the simple 'do's' and 'don'ts', for the stranger then feels comfortable and is not likely (at least knowingly) to give offence. Australia is a very relaxed country, but a few tips may prove useful.

Table manners follow the British pattern rather than the American where the food is only eaten with a fork after the knife has done its job. Similarly at the end of a meal the knife and fork are placed together, side by side in the centre of the plate. In that way the waiter or your host or hostess know that you have finished eating, although it is only when all the diners have finished will the whole table be cleared and the next course served. If the waiter sees the cutlery on the side of the plate, he presumes that the diner is being polite and resting between mouthfuls. The different ways of handling cutlery often causes confusion and lead people needlessly to think that the service is slow.

It is worth noting that in restaurants the word 'entrée' is used meaning a starter and as Australia makes some fine cheeses these are often served as a separate course, not just as 'nibbles' in the American manner with drinks before the meal.

To complicate matters further, the cheese (usually a selection) is either served in the French manner before desert, enabling you to finish your red wine or at the end of the meal with an Australian port. Incidentally these ports are rarely exported and certainly not as port, as only those made in Portugal can be classed as such for export purposes.

Coffee is always served at the end of the meal and not with desert unless requested. However, if you do not feel like eating a large meal of many courses, 'grazing' or having two entrées or an entrée and two deserts or whatever combination that appeals is perfectly acceptable. Indeed, many innovative restaurants take this into consideration and often you can order a course served as either a large or small portion. This makes for a relaxed and enjoyable evening as well as ensuring that you eat exactly the amount you wish to.

When dining out dress is usually of the smart casual variety, but if in doubt always ask. If travelling in the winter months, remember that although never really cold (apart from the ski-resorts), Australians, unlike Americans and Northern Europeans, do not generally invest in central heating and consequently usually wear layers of warm clothing. This is especially important to remember if visiting private homes in winter.

A gift is always appreciated by the host or hostess when invited to a meal in their home. Wine (you can always ask advice in the local bottle shop who will only be too happy to guide you in your selection) or flowers which are invariably extremely well presented by florists, making them almost into works of art at times. If possible, ask for some 'natives' to be included in the flower arrangement. Australian native flowers are not only striking and unusual in appearance, but long-lasting as well. Your hostess will be delighted by your insight into Australian horticulture.

If by any chance you have misunderstood the invitation or time did not allow you to purchase a gift, flowers can always be sent the next day with a suitable Thank You note. Indeed, although not obligatory, it is a very nice idea to send a hand-written note the next day thanking your hosts for their hospitality. You can of course telephone, but a short note will not only be appreciated, but clearly shows your gratitude in that you have taken the time and made the effort to pick up a pen rather than a phone.

Hot Tip: Never Arrive Early for Lunch or Dinner

Never arrive early for a lunch or dinner party. Ten to fifteen minutes after the stated time is preferred.

If taking a taxi in either Melbourne or Sydney, make certain at the beginning that the taxi driver knows where the address is. If staying at an hotel enlist the bell-captain's help before stepping into the taxi. For many taxi drivers this is their first job after entering Australia, so they may not be familiar with your English and/or the location, if it is not in the middle of the city.

Nineteenth-century terraced houses, Paddington, Sydney

The Australian 'Barbie'

The 'barbie' is of course a very relaxed affair and it is more than likely that some of the guests will be wearing the ubiquitous shorts and 'thongs' or flip-flops. Timing is always elastic. Remember that it takes time for the 'barbie' to heat up and so it may be some time after your arrival before the food is cooked. As well as the excellent grilled meats (be sure to tell you hosts if you are vegetarian or vegan), fish and shell-fish, you will probably also be served a selection of wonderful salads to accompany the meal with all manner of ingredients and dressings. A delightful Aussie way to be entertained.

Do not hesitate to introduce yourself. Australians like the American approach of an outstretched hand and your name, rather than the more diffident British approach of standing back and waiting to be introduced to people before you can start a conversation. Indeed, Australians might think you are aloof and perhaps a bit snobby if you adopt the latter approach.

The 'barbie'

To obtain money while you are in Oz, if you have a Mastercard, Visa or American Express and a personal identification number (PIN) you can use automatic teller machines in the cities. You can buy phone cards from newsagents and post offices (which are often quite grand buildings) from 9.00am to 5.00pm Monday to Friday. The egalitarian tradition is fiercely adhered to in these places as queuing or standing in line is mandatory. Woe-betide the person who thinks that he or she can jump the queue. An unforgivable sin!

Hot Tip: The Tipping Technique

Due to the egalitarian spirit tipping is not the minefield that it is in other countries. It is an unwritten law in Oz that a lone male passenger always sits up front next to the driver, while the female sits at the back. Tipping is seen as being given for good service. Typically, you would expect to tip around 10% in a restaurant, 15% if the service was particularly good. A service charge is not usually included in the bill and as far as the taxi drivers are concerned they appreciate it if you round up the fare to the nearest dollar.

7

Sport & Outdoor Life

'Aussies play to win'

Never mind the laid back attitude in Oz, sport is serious stuff! Everybody participates, spectates and has an opinion on it. Acres of newsprint and hours of TV are devoted to it. Aussies play to win, nobody remembers the person who came second and sporting triumphs are matters of great national pride. The climate certainly helps, plus the availability of every type of sport including even ski-ing in the winter months. The fact that most of the population lives near the coastal fringe means that water sports are also easily available and very popular.

Some sports are unique to Australia or more accurately Victoria, which is the home of Aussie Rules Football. It is fanatically followed in this state and its supporters embrace all ages and sexes, making it very much a family sport. South Australia and Western Australia are also mad about 'footy'. It has its origins in Gaelic football, the sport the early migrants from Ireland brought with them. New South Wales and Queensland, however, are devoted to Rugby League, the historical legacy of those who come from northern industrialized England, although it is fair to say that Aussie Rules is gaining in popularity in New South Wales and Queensland.

Cricket is a national passion, played and enjoyed country-wide during the summer months. The sunshine and the beer being very much part of the sport. Of course the Test Series against the 'Poms' (the English) or the 'Windies' (West Indies) are keenly followed. Despite being a team sport, cricketing heroes are larger-than-life individuals and achieve cult status.

As well as the two-legged heroes, there are also the four-legged ones. Horse racing is extremely popular: the whole country effectively comes to a standstill when the Melbourne Cup is run on the first Tuesday in November; moreover, in Victoria the day is a public holiday. It is the greatest racing and social event (complete with outrageous hats!) in Australia and a marvellous event to attend. Perhaps the 'Trots' are more to your liking. Do not be alarmed, for these are the very popular pony-trap races and great fun to watch.

Bush-walking is a great way for the visitor to experience at first hand the uniqueness of Australia's plant and animal life. The National Parks all have excellent visitor centres providing plenty of information on the terrain and the type of walk you want to do. It is essential to go properly prepared and to tell people where you are going.

Hot Tip: Be Careful of the Sun!

The danger of Australia's wildlife is greatly exaggerated and no doubt you will hear horror stories of shark and crocodile attacks. The fact is that the greatest danger the visitor is likely to encounter is the sun. It is certainly a force to be reckoned with and respected and a few simple but necessary precautions will allow you to enjoy the sunshine as well as not endangering your health.

'Slip, slap, slop' has become an Aussie Government slogan over the last few years. Alarmed by the rise in the number of skin cancers caused by the sun, a huge, national advertising campaign was launched to make the public aware of the dangers of the sun. Paler is safer in Oz today and 'slip, slap, slop' refers to the sound of a T-shirt being put on, a hat slapped on your head and finally the sound of sun cream being applied. It has been a popular, successful campaign, but the visitor should not be too complacent and conveyed into a false sense of security after applying sun protection. Sun creams help prevent burning but be careful of what strong sun can still do to your skin. Total sun blocks are probably the answer especially if you have a fair skin. Having a good pair of sunglasses is an essential, as is wearing a wide-brimmed hat for both men and women.

When bush-walking make certain that you stick to the tracks, wear walking shoes or boots and suitable clothing. It is a good idea to wear long trousers or socks to minimize the risks of snake bites and ticks when walking in long undergrowth.

Life on the ocean waves

Just as humans appreciate sunshine and warmth, so do the creepy-crawlies! They can be a nuisance during the summer and it is a good idea to go equipped with a good insect repellent. It is unlikely that you will encounter the infamous funnel-web spider found on Sydney's north shore or the redback found in dry, dark locations but, if you do, give them a wide berth!

A more realistic threat comes from the jelly-fish found in the warm, tropical waters off the Queensland coast and elsewhere in summer. Some beaches have bottles of vinegar to apply to stings.

WHAT TO WEAR

In the Australian Summer which begins in November and continues through to the end of March it is very warm-to-hot everywhere. In the tropical north it rains a great deal, is humid and thunderstorms occasionally occur. Cotton casual clothes are ideal, as are comfortable flat shoes or sandals. Melbourne's temperature can go from 10° to 30+° Celsius (50° to 85+° Fahrenheit) in one day and Sydney becomes humid in the middle of summer, but refreshing southerly winds in the evenings are wonderful.

Hot Tip: New Arrivals Should Take It Easy!

It is a good idea to give yourself a leisurely first day or two after arriving in Australia in summer, because apart from jet-lag, if you are visiting from the northern hemisphere, your body is geared up for winter.

Winters in Australia are short – from June through to the end of August. Sydney is still reasonably mild, but the temperature can drop in Melbourne and Southern Australia generally, and so a lightweight coat and warmer clothing is recommended. Northern Australia has warm-to-hot days, is fairly dry, especially areas like those featured in *Crocodile Dundee*. It can be fairly cool in the evenings and inland nights are often surprisingly cold. You need to be 'rugged up'.

8

Walkabout

Uluru – Ayres Rock

It is a self-evident truth that there is a lot to see in Australia. Most people over-plan their trips, but this is one country where some forward planning pays dividends. Think about how much time you can spend in Oz and prioritize what you want to see. Is it the breathtaking coral reefs, the vast outback, the sandy beaches, the magnificent rain forests or perhaps the lively Sydney scene? The choice is almost overwhelming.

In whichever city you first arrive, it is a good idea to give yourself a couple of days to reorientate and allow your body time to adjust – both from the jet-lag and the difference in seasons – especially if you are travelling from the Northern hemisphere.

The first few days would allow you to explore, say the historic Rocks area in Sydney, the Domain, perhaps a harbour cruise and a visit to the Opera House. Think about going to the Opera, a concert or play depending on the season and the availability of tickets and treat yourself to supper afterwards in one of the restaurants overlooking the harbour. A truly memorable evening.

If in Melbourne, Australia's second largest city, a trip on one of the trams to the sea-side area of St Kilda (wonderful pastry shops in Acland Street); a visit to the recently-opened opulent casino with its designer shops, presumably for those who win at the tables; a stroll beside the Yarra River at Southgate and a meal in one of the many excellent restaurants will give you a real feel for the city. Incidentally, both Sydney and Melbourne have truly magnificent Botanical Gardens for those moments when you want to get away from people and be soothed by some greenery.

If you want to see what the great houses of nineteenth-century Melbourne looked like, a visit to Como House is most rewarding. The elegant white mansion, furnished largely in the period style, is located in the fashionable suburb of South Yarra. Note the kitchen located away from the house. The fear of fire was a constant threat. Lindsay

House in Sydney is another example and after absorbing nineteenth-century detail, you might like to visit the nearby expensive suburb of Double Bay or 'Double Pay' as the locals call it, and watch the fashionable Sydney-siders go by, while sipping a 'latte'.

SHOPPING

If shopping is your vice, then the Queen Victoria Building, as well as the delightful quaint Strand Arcade in Sydney, offer not only a wide selection but some fascinating speciality and off-beat shops as well. In Melbourne, the oldest arcade of all, the Royal Arcade, is adorned with the seven-foot statues of Gog and Magog that strike the clock on the hour. The Block Arcade, so-called because of the tradition of walking around the fashionable streets or 'doing the block', is splendid – with its marble floor, pillars and glass roof. It has lovely old-fashioned tea-rooms for when you are in need of refreshment.

Hot Tip: Check Opening Times

Historic houses are open at different times, depending on the season. It is always worth double-checking before you set out.

For a more modern approach, a visit to 'Australia on Collins' in Melbourne is an eye-opener. Here you will find modern Australian fashion, bookshops, design shops as well as all types of opal jewellery in shops nearby. The latter are tax-free for tourists, but do shop around to compare quality and prices.

HUNTER VALLEY & GREAT OCEAN ROAD

Venturing beyond both cities opens up more vistas. From Sydney the famous wine-growing area of the Hunter Valley is within easy reach, as are the Royal National Park and Blue Mountains. The latter are especially good if you want to get some experience of the bush and vastness of Australia, albeit in microcosm.

From Melbourne different excursions can be organized. A trip to Healsville, the wildlife sanctuary north of Melbourne in the Dandenong Ranges, takes a few hours and there you can see the diversity of Australian native wildlife. Do not, however, mention the well-intentioned import of many European and North American species, let alone domestic pets. These have sadly ravaged

Melbourne trams

some of Australia's most vulnerable species. The domestic cat is seen as the greatest villain of the piece today, especially so if it becomes feral.

In the other direction, a trip along the Great Ocean Road, one of the huge public works projects in the 1930s and like the Sydney Harbour Bridge, is now one of the country's great tourist attractions. The 300km (180 miles) of the Great Ocean Road take you through some spectacular scenery, as it follows the coves, bluffs and promontories of Victoria's coastline. There are some good surfing beaches and appealing towns en route should you wish to explore a little more.

Coach trips can easily be arranged, often through your hotel or for the more budget-conscious a visit to the kiosk in Burke Street in Melbourne might lead to a heavily discounted ticket, especially if you decide to take a tour at the last minute. The same also holds true for theatre and concert tickets.

Many places can easily be reached from Melbourne in a day, by train from either

Perth skyline

Spencer or Flinders Street stations. The latter's famous clocks are still there over the front of the station after a public campaign to stop development plans altering the station façade. For this is the most famous meeting place for Melburnians.

Mornington Peninsula would be a great place to visit especially out of season. During summer weekends the beaches are packed. Philip Island nearby is a year round attraction, for there every night you can see hundreds of fairy penguins waddle ashore. The more adventurous traveller might like to hire a car and travel independently. If this is the case it is a good idea to book in advance especially if your visit is in the peak holiday months.

Hot Tip: Watch the Speed Limit!

Driving is on the left hand side of the road with a maximum speed limit in cities and towns of 60 km/h (35 mph) and 100 km/h (62 mph) on country roads and highways unless signs indicate otherwise.

Australia has been fully metric for many years, so all distances are expressed in kilometres. It is worth remembering, too, that Australia was the first country to make the wearing of seat belts compulsory; it is taken very seriously. Also taken very seriously are the drink-driving laws, with random breath checks being conducted regularly in most states. Do not be surprised by the police breathalizing people on their way to work in the morning, as alcohol levels after a hard night's drinking take time to drop and the police are aware of this.

The koala bear – a national symbol

If travelling in the outback, plan your trip with the aid of a good map and of course check conditions and facilities before your departure. Always carry ample supplies of petrol, food and water and stay on recognized routes as well as heed warnings about the possibility of bush fires.

TRAVELLING BY TRAIN

If you would like the train to take more of the strain, there are several long distance trains, some of which have been extensively renovated and refurbished. These offer first class, deluxe and economy class compartments complete with sleeping berths, showers, buffet and dining cars. These trains are a wonderful old-fashioned travelling experience, but with all modern comforts.

Enquire about the flexible rail passes such as Austrail Pass, Austrail Flexipass and the East Coast Discovery Pass. To obtain the best possible discounts they must be purchased outside the country. You can usually break your journey on these trains, providing that you have indicated this at the time of purchase, but the journey must be completed within a specified time.

The two most memorable train journeys are on the *Indian Pacific* and the *Ghan*; the latter is Australia's most prestigious and luxurious train. The *Indian Pacific* is so called, because it crosses the continent from Sydney and the Pacific, to Perth on the Indian Ocean. The trip takes two days and three nights. What an epic journey!

From Sydney the train heads out towards the Blue Mountains to Lithgow and then into rural Australia. It crosses the South Australian border and on to Adelaide. The wheat country is next. The journey swings westwards into the famous 'long straight' 478km (270 miles) of unbending track. The train eventually crosses the border into Western Australia and on to Kalgoorie. Then its through the vast wheat belt, finally arriving in Perth. Seasonal and discount fares are available so it is worth enquiring before booking.

The *Ghan* runs twice a week for most of the year and departs from Adelaide taking one day and one night. Adelaide, incidentally, hosts Australia's most famous literary festival every two years. South Australia indeed is proud of its heritage, the fact that it has always been a 'free state' meaning that there were never any convicts and free settlers were sold small units of land, being guaranteed religious and civil liberties from the beginning.

By travelling on the *Ghan* you could explore Australia's 'Red Centre', using the Anangu Tours. The Anangu people organize guided tours explaining the culture and traditions of the Aboriginals in that part of Australia, together with teaching bush-survival skills. These are the custodians of Uluru – formerly known as Ayres Rock.

The *Ghan*

Queensland offers the *Spirit of the Outback* train as well as the *Queenslander*, which heads north from Brisbane to tropical Cairns. For the latest in train luxury, the *Great South Pacific Express* would take some beating. The train, brand new but modelled on a design of 1902, recreates the age of elegant travel and takes you from Sydney to Cairns with side trips to the Great Barrier Reef, the world's longest living organism, and the rain forest. In the Reef there are islands to suit every taste and budget from the family-oriented island of Dunk to the two most exclusive and expensive islands, Lizard and Bedarra. Perhaps you would like to see where the rain forest and reef meet at Cape Tribulation, so called when Captain Cook's vessel hit a reef in 1770. You have been warned!

TRAVELLING BY PLANE

There are of course domestic flights within Australia and regional airlines can fly you to just about anywhere you want to go. Again, do enquire about domestic flights from your travel agent. Quantas, for example, offers packages consisting of a return inter-continental flight plus a number of domestic flights for an overall fixed sum. These packages offer real savings and are well worth investigating.

When visiting Northern Queensland and the Northern Territory you may find it useful to contact one of the many smaller airline companies, if you are interested in visiting some of the more out-of-the-way places. There is nothing more exhilarating than flying in a small light aircraft gazing down at the vastness of Australia beneath you.

If visiting the Northern Territory and Kakadu National Park where much of *Crocodile Dundee* was filmed, remember that although it is cooler in June, July and August, it is also very dry, with parched brown earth and consequently few animals to be seen. Summer is hot, but wet and a much better time to see the animal life.

FESTIVALS

Another great feature of Australia worth remembering on your visit are the number of great festivals held each year. The Christmas and Easter holiday periods are especially good times to catch up with a festival somewhere, starting with the Sydney mid-summer festival in January and going on to the biggest Gay festival in the world, the Sydney Gay and Lesbian Mardi Gras. It finishes with an extravagant parade which used to be filmed by the ABC (Australian Broadcasting Corporation) but now there are edited highlights only!

Sydney Opera House

Perhaps the most innovative Arts Festival is held every two years (in even years) during March in Adelaide. Staying in the same region of South Australia but held in odd years, the Barossa Valley Vintage Festival celebrates the regions' wines and its Germanic heritage.

Melbourne, not to be outdone, hosts an International Film Festival in June and an International Festival of Arts in October. Indeed, all the state capitals are anxious to promote the arts and regularly have celebratory showcase festivals.

Whatever you decide to do, it will be 'beaut'.

9

Australian Speak

Merino sheep on an outback property

Considering it is such a huge country, it is surprising that Australia has no regional dialects or differences in pronunciation. The strong Australian accent is referred to as 'Broad Strine' (think of Paul Hogan in *Crocodile Dundee* or Dame Edna Everidge), but most people in the cities speak what is becoming known as 'General Australian'. Thus, the visitor will have few problems.

Do not confuse Australian with New Zealand English; granted, it can be difficult to tell the difference at times to the un-tuned ear. Indeed, there is reference to Southern Hemisphere English in academic circles and if you listen to Australian, New Zealand and even South African English (as distinct from Afrikaans English) you can detect a distinct similarity, especially in the vowel sounds. Australians would disagree and state that the Kiwi's (New Zealanders') pronunciation is certainly different from that of an Aussie. New Zealanders, they point out, say 'Yiss' for 'Yes' and a major thoroughfare in Sydney, Pitt Street becomes a domesticated animal to a Kiwi, as it is transformed into 'Pet Street'. An Australian butcher is amused by New Zealanders ordering six of anything, as in 'Sex Sausages'!

ART OF BREVITY

Australians admire brevity, especially in speech. In order to achieve this they have shortened many words in the English language to end in either 'o' or 'ie', as in postie – postman, journo – journalist. So you might overhear a conversation along the lines of:

> 'Yesterday arvo, the poli was wrapt with his new ute. Today he felt crook and thought of taking a sickie, when he read the journo's article on the goss, saying that he was involved in a rort.'

The translation of the above is:

'Yesterday afternoon, the politician was delighted with his new pick-up truck. Today he felt ill and thought of taking a day's sick leave when he read the journalist's article concerning the gossip that he was involved in a scam.'

If the original Aussie version was read aloud, the speaker would lift their voice at the end of each sentence. Be warned this habit becomes quite infectious even after a short stay in Australia and especially when speaking to someone on the telephone.

LONDON COCKNEYS

Australian English has its origins in the English that came with the early convicts, many of whom were London cockneys, as well as those coming from the rest of Britain and Ireland. Some words in current use today in Australia are pure nineteenth-century English, while others have been adapted from the original Australian.

The only regional difference perhaps is that Queenlanders are supposed to speak more slowly than other Australians. However, if you stay at Queensland tourist resorts you will probably find that the waiting, front of house staff, diving instructors and others all hail from the rest of Australia. Queensland is a magnet, especially to those from Victoria in the winter.

Australian Vocab

The popularity of Australian films and soap-operas like 'Neighbours' has made some of the following words and colourful phrases familiar, but a knowledge and revision of the following might prove useful:

Bathers – swimming costume
Bonzer – enjoyable or excellent, somewhat old-fashioned now. **Ripper** is more up to date
Bludger – somebody who avoids work and responsibilities, often used in 'dole bludger', somebody who lives off the state's unemployment benefits when in reality they could get a job
Bottle Shop – wine shop, off-licence, liquor store
Chook – chicken
Compo – compensation
Crook – sick or ill
Dag – literally one of the locks of wool clotted with dirt about the hind portions of a sheep. Used as a derogatory term about a person.
Do a Uee – do a U-Turn

Dob In – to inform on someone and get them into trouble
Dunny – outside lavatory, a legendary item in Australian humour
Esky – portable cooling box for carrying beer and wine
Good on Yer (them) – good for you
Grog – alcoholic drink
Jackaroo – worker on a sheep or cattle station in the outback
Jarmies – pyjamas
Layby – purchase by instalments
Larrikin – mischievous youth, scallywag
Ocker – previously used to describe an average Australian man now an Extreme Australian, often boorish and jingoistic as in the 'Ugly Ocker'
Pashing – kissing
Plunger – a cafetière
Prezzie – a present
Pokies – poker machines
Ratbag – ultimate derogatory description of a person
Roo Bar – bull bar. Metal fixture at the front of a car to limit damage done to a car, if it comes into collision with a kangaroo (Roo). These are a real problem if driving in the country at night, as these heavy animals are attracted and dazzled by a car's headlights
Sheila – old slang expression for a woman
Sticky Beak – a nosey, inquisitive person
Strides – trousers
Tazzie – Tasmania

'Throw a wobbly' – loose your temper/have a tantrum
Uni – university
Unit – flat or apartment
Whinger – somebody who complains as in the infamous 'whinging Pom'. Pom being not a very complimentary name for an Englishman and probably comes from convict days as in Prisoner of His Majesty – P.O.M.
Woop-Woop/Back of Burke – a term to describe somewhere deep in the outback. The former being used in New South Wales and the latter in Victoria and elsewhere.
Wowser – a killjoy
Youse – you, as in 'Youse better be rugged up', you had better dress warmly
'You scrub up well' – you look very well dressed

Hot Tip: Do Not be Offended by the Language

One note of advice, many words in British or American English which would be considered swearing are perfectly acceptable in Australia and are sometimes seen as words of endearment such as 'Bastard' and 'Bugger'; and 'bloody' is an everyday adjective. So do not be offended.

The word 'mate' has real meaning in Australian, especially in the bush where it is hard work either on a sheep or cattle station, both in terms of the climate and the physical work. You need to rely there on other people sometimes for survival itself so mateship is very important.

You will hear Australians using the term mate to each other both in the city and the bush, but visitors to Australia should avoid striking a false note by referring to Australian colleagues, friends and especially acquaintances as 'mate'. They may not regard you as such!

The macho, rough and tough image can still be found in the outback for reasons already explained above, but most Australians, especially young Australians, believe in equality and freedom of opportunity for all individuals, no matter what their race, religion or gender is, so no jokes about 'Sheilas'! The Bruce and Sheila Australian stereotypes, if they ever existed, have long since disappeared.

The kangaroo ('roo') – unique to Australia

Further Reading

Here are a few ideas for those who are interested in digging a little deeper and finding out more about Australia. Everything from class in Australia (is there such an outmoded élitist attitude in Oz?) through history, fiction, modern Australian cooking and interior design.

History and Contemporary Affaires

A Concise History of Australia by Russell Ward
A Shorter History of Australia by Geoffrey Blainey

Both are informative without being too academic.

Damned Whores and God's Police by Ann Summers

This is a very different read. The title is meant to shock and reflects the attitude of the authorities to both female convicts and female free settlers. Summers goes on to explore the influence that this perception has had on the status, treatment and influence of women, not only in the colony, but also in modern Australia as well.

Rivers of Blood, Rivers of Gold by Mark Cocker

The story of Aborigines in Tasmania.

A Secret Country by John Pilger

This is a thought-provoking book about the other side of the 'lucky country' in recent times.

Class in Australia by Craig McGregor

Something of an eye-opener for those who believe that Australia is a classless society. In this controversial book McGregor examines the origins of the social divisions in Australian society today.

Fiction

There is a wealth of modern Australian literature and here are just a few examples:

Johnno and anything else by David Malouf
Batchelor Kisses by Nick Earls
Sound of One Hand Clapping by Richard Flanagan
Death of a River Guide by Richard Flanagan
Three Dollars by Elliot Perlman
Vanity Fierce by Graeme Aitken
Night Letters by Robert Dessaix
The Chosen by David Ireland
Praise and *1988* by Andrew McGahan
French Mathematician by Tom Petsinis
Oscar and Lucinda by Peter Carey
Charades by Janette Turner Hospital
My Father's Moon by Elizabeth Jolley
Amy's Children by Olga Masters
The Riders by Tim Winton
Chant of Jimmy Blacksmith by Thomas Keneally
For Love Alone by Christina Stead

Humour

Let's Talk Strine by Alferbeck Lavder
They're a Weird Mob by Nino Culotta

Biography

Snake Crade and *Snake Dancing* by Roberta Sykes

The author is part Aboriginal. It is only fair to point out that the books have drawn adverse critism from some sections of the Aboriginal community.

Interior Design

Inside Australia Interiors by Janne Faulkner

A fascinating look at the Aussie innovative use of all that light and space, while concentrating on the idea that rooms should flow into one another and not be limited to just one purpose.

Modern Australian Cooking

There are a large number of excellent books on the subject. Here are a few of the most popular:

New Cook and *New Entertaining* by Donna Hay
Favourite Food and *New Food* by Jill Duplaix
The Cook's Companion and *Recipes My Mother Gave Me* by Stephanie Alexander
Maggie's Orchard and *Maggies's Farm* by Margaret Beer

Eating Out in Sydney and Melbourne

The Sydney Morning Herald Good Food Guide
The Age Good Food Guide (Melbourne)

Both are reliable, informative guides for exploring the delights of eating out in both cities and the surrounding areas.

Facts About Australia

Geography and climate

Australia has a land area of 7.7m square kilometres (nearly 3m square miles) and is the smallest of the planet's five continents – or as some would describe it, the largest island (the 'South Land'). Despite its huge size and dependence on rural production, it is one of the most urbanized countries in the world, with two-thirds of the population living in the eight biggest cities, all but one of them – the federal capital of Canberra – being situated on the coast.

The land mass is mostly flat and empty, extending for hundreds of miles without interruption. There are exceptions, such as at the edges of the many plateaux, which make up the continent, where deep gorges and waterfalls create spectacular rugged relief between the Great Divide and the coast. The most mountainous area is found in the east (between Melbourne and Brisbane), including Tasmania, where the majority of the population lives.

The highest summits in the east are Mt Kosciusko (2,230m, 7,314 ft), Round Mountain (1,615m, 5,297 ft) and Bartle Frere (l,611m, 5,287ft).

Australia also has its own ski resorts in the Snowy Moutains (part of the Great Dividing Range) within 400km (250 miles) of both Sydney and Melbourne.

The moderating influence of the surrounding oceans means that the climate is less subject to extremes than regions of comparable size in other parts of the world. Thus, Australian deserts are only moderately arid, hence the widespread vegetation cover. (Despite great variations from year to year and season to season, no Australian climate station records a mean annual rainfall below 10mm – 4″.)

The most adaptable tree genus in Australia is the Eucalypts with over 600 species (Eucalyptus), which ranges from the tall flooded gum trees found on the edges of the rain forest in south- western Australia, the great jarrah forests of Eucalyptus hardwoods, to the dry-living mallee (scrub) species found on sand-plains and dunes.

The continent is host to nearly 300 different mammals, 400 species of reptiles and 700 birds. Aboriginals arriving from Asia over 50,000 years ago brought the dingo.

The Kanagaroo – Australia's best known Marsupial

Australia has a great many marsupials. Best known are the big red and grey kangaroos, that range over the dry grasslands and forests across the continent; standing 2 metres (6′6″) tall, they now compete for food with cattle and sheep. They bound along at speed (15km – 9-10 miles per hour) and can clear fences of their own height. Wallabies, a smaller species of the same family, live in the forests and mountains. There are over 60 different species of kangaroo and wallaby. The population of the four most common kind is estimated to be 50 million, or nearly three times the human population of the continent.

Also well known are the koala bears that live in trees and feed exclusively off Eucalyptus leaves. Another notable marsuptial is the ground-burrowing wombat that feeds in the undergrowth and behaves like a giant rodent.

There are 18,000 species of flowering plants in Australia, 15,000 of them are found nowhere else in the world.

Drive on the Left

Vehicles are driven on the left in Australia; also, like the UK, electricity is 220 volts.

No large predators – but. . .

Although Australia lacks large land predators like the lion, bear and tiger, it makes up for it with a huge assortment of other dangerous creatures. There are large crocodiles in the north, venomous spiders and snakes (some of the most dangerous of both) throughout the country, and sharks appear off the entire coast of Australia (36,000km – 22500 miles), though shark attacks on humans are rare. What is far more common is the painful and sometimes fatal sting of the stonefish as well as various types of jellyfish.

Great Barrier Reef

This is a maze of some 2500 reefs off the north-east coast of Australia, exposed only at low tide, ranging in size from a few hundred hectares to 50 sq.km (20 sq.miles), and extending over an area of 250,000 sq.km (100,000 sq.miles). Most notable is the section north of Cairns, which extends for about 800km (500 miles). Today, much of the reef is protected within the Great Barrier Reef Marine Park. Most National Parks in Australia are World Heritage sites.

Mineral Resources

Much of Australia, it seems, is one vast great mineral reserve. Not surprisingly, much of the country's growth since the beginning of European settlement has been closely related to the exploitation of such resources, which has led directly to the building and often eventual decline of the majority of inland towns.

Broken Hill and Mount Isa are copper, lead, zinc and silver-producing centres, while Kalgoorlie, Bendigo, Ballarat and Charter Towers all grew in the middle and late nineteenth-century gold rushes. Today, the heavy industrial minerals of Western Australia, such as the huge iron ore mines of Mount Tom Price, Mount Newman and Mount Goldsworthy are fundamental to the Australian economy, as is coal: Australia is the world's biggest exporter of coal and diamonds.

Also important are the offshore oil and gas fields of the north-west shelf. In addition, in the north and east is coal and bauxite. More recently, uranium is being mined in Darwin and further east. New mineral discoveries are taking place all the time.

Australia is now more than self-sufficient in all foods.

The continent is divided into the states of New South Wales, Queensland (1859), South Australia (1825), Victoria (1851) and Western Australia (1829), The area now forming the Northern Territory (formerly under the control of South Australia) has been self-governing since 1978. During the colonial period the state sea-port capitals of Sydney, Brisbane, Adelaide, Hobart, Melbourne and Perth (today accounting for over 60% of Australia's population of 18m) became established as the dominant manufacturing, commercial and administrative and legislative centres of their respective states.

In 1901, the states came together to create the Commonwealth of Australia with a federal constitution.

The federal capital established at Canberra, in the new Australian Capital Territory, south of Sydney, has grown from being a tiny settlement in 1911 to becoming a major city today.

The National Anthem is *Advance Australia Fair* – based on a nineteenth-century patriotic song. It was officially adopted in 1984 after several referenda in which it came ahead of *Waltzing Matilda*.

The national colours of the country used in sporting events are green and gold.

Australia is the largest per capita share-owning society in the world. One half of the adult population own shares in publicly-listed companies.

Australia's flag

The Australian flag has a royal blue background with five white stars [the Southern Cross] on the right, a large white seven-pointed star [the Federation star] on the bottom of the left-hand corner and the Union flag of Great Britain on the top left-hand corner. The latter represents Australia's historical links with Britain, the Federation star represents Australia's six states and its territories, while the Southern Cross is a feature of the Southern Hemisphere sky at night.

There is a written constitution clearly defining the roles of the federal and states' governments, and any changes to the constitution have to be brought about by referendum.

A quarter of Australia's population was born overseas, and while English is the official language, Italian is the most widely taught second language.

Australia was the first country in the world to have a complete system of bank notes made of plastic. These last four times as long as paper notes and are more difficult to counterfeit.

It is said that it is difficult for people from Europe or North America to appreciate the sheer size and emptiness of Australia. For example, Perth – the capital of Western Australia – qualifies as the most isolated city in the world. It is 2700km (about 1700 miles) from its closest neighbour, Adelaide – capital of South Australia – further than from London to Moscow or New York to Denver.

The Australian flag

Index